Outdoor
LIV
OUTDOORS

David Watkins and Meike Dalal

Illustrated by Jonathan Langley
Designed by Sally Burrough
Edited by Bridget Gibbs

About the authors

David Watkins is an art lecturer and is the Organizing Secretary of Breakaway, an organization staffed entirely by unpaid camping enthusiasts who arrange and run camping holidays and other outdoor activities for children from the age of seven upwards.
Meike Dalal is a junior school teacher and is also on the staff of Breakaway.
Both have been involved in camping, youth hostelling, cycling and walking since childhood, and have run camps all over Britain and also in Europe.

Special Consultant
Peter C. Nicholls, author and lecturer in outdoor education; Chairman, Physical Activities Panel, the Duke of Edinburgh's Award in Australia.

First published in 1979 by Usborne Publishing Ltd., 20 Garrick Street, London WC2E 9BJ, England.

Published in Canada by Hayes Publishing Ltd., Burlington, Ontario.

Printed in England by Waterlow (Dunstable) Ltd.

Contents

About camping

This book is an introduction to camping and the fun that can be had from living outdoors. Many people think that a lot of expensive equipment is needed for camping, but this is not true. It is quite easy to camp safely using ordinary household items and only a little special equipment.

This book is intended as a guide to help you get started. Once you have gained experience, you will discover your own ways of doing things.

Later on, you may want to become adventurous and camp in extreme conditions such as mountains, deserts or heathlands. But remember, this should not be attempted without expert guidance and until you have had a lot of experience of camping.

How to start

If your house has a garden, you can start by camping out overnight with a friend. You will be amazed at the noises you notice and the change in the temperature.

If you go on holiday with your parents, you could camp while they stay in a hotel or caravan. It would be cheaper for them and more fun for you.

When you have some experience of camping, look for sites on private land not too far from home where you can camp for a weekend.

As you gain more experience, you can safely camp further away from home and stay for longer periods. Always make sure to tell your parents where you are going.

Before you go camping you should do some cooking. Practise at home in the kitchen to find out which dishes are easiest to make.

If possible, cook in the garden with a camp stove and make a list of things you use. You can't pop back into the kitchen when camping.

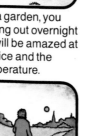

Finding and choosing a site

Before you pick a site, think about the kind of place you want to camp in and what you want to do there. You might want to be near the sea or near good walking country, or you might want to go bird-watching. Let your interests guide you.

First look at a map of the area you have chosen, to try and spot possible sites. If you can, visit the area before you go camping.

It is a good idea to travel through the area by train, as you may see sites that are not easily accessible from a road.

You can see more from a bus than a car because it's higher up. So if you can't get a train, look around the area on a local bus.

If you are cycling, stop and ask local people about possible sites. As a last resort, you could look at a book of camp sites.

When you have found a site, first see if you can get permission to camp there from the owner. If he agrees, you can then go and select the best position to camp.

Start by trying to imagine the site under the worst possible weather conditions. If you are able to, visit it in the depths of winter.

Select a level site, not one at the bottom of a slope. It might rain.

If you camp on a slope, you will wake up at one end of your tent, or outside it.

Choose a place away from cliffs or trees to avoid falling objects.

Look for a sheltered site, near bushes or a bank.

Consider the distance between the site and the nearest water supply.

Try to avoid a site downwind from farm animal buildings, because of the smell.

Look for signs that tell you which way the wind usually blows, e.g. trees bent over.

A good position to pitch your tent is on a raised area. It is quite likely to be the driest site and it will be the one with the best view.

Look for signs of marshy ground, such as plants that normally live in wet areas. A site near stagnant water will attract biting insects.

Never camp in a dry gully. Whole expeditions have been swept away by sudden floods.

Types of camp: standing . . .

Before you go camping, you need to decide how long you are going for and what kind of camp you want it to be. There are two main types of camp, called standing and lightweight camps.

A standing camp is one in which you pitch your tent on one site for the whole camp. The position of the site is particularly important as the camp will be a base from which to go out for day trips.

When you first go camping, it is best to start with short standing camps to get experience. If you go for a weekend you can easily take with you all the food and clothing you will need. A longer camp needs more planning. You will have to consider washing clothes, and if you are not camping near shops, you will need a larger store of food. You will also need to make proper toilet facilities and to think about what you will do with rubbish.

When you choose a standing camp site, try to consider everyone's interests. Aim to mix visits to towns and museums with trips to the river or sea.

... and lightweight

Lightweight camping is for those who like to travel around, staying only one or two nights at each site. As the name suggests, the idea is to keep weight to a minimum, as it is no fun hiking with a heavy rucksack. You take only the most essential equipment, and it must be as light and compact as possible.

This kind of camping is not really suitable for beginners. You must be skilled at pitching your tent quickly in any weather and you must be able to use a map and compass for finding your way.

If you do go lightweight camping, it is best to go with a friend. You will be able to share equipment, such as the tent and cooking pots, so that you have less to carry. But make sure each of you always carries some food and water in case you ever get separated or lost.

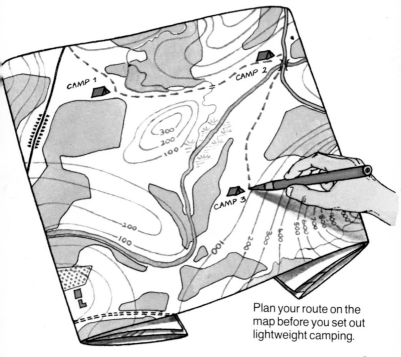

Plan your route on the map before you set out lightweight camping.

9

Clothing

What you need to take depends on where you go camping and the time of year. The pictures on the left page show some of the clothes you will need in cold and wet weather. Those on the right show some you need for hot, dry weather.

There are some clothes which you always need to take. These are: underwear,

Waterproof jacket with hood.
Jeans or **trousers,** two pairs.
Stout shoes; take walking boots if you intend to do a lot of walking.
Woolly socks, four pairs; wear two pairs with walking shoes.

Jumpers, two of medium thickness, and preferably made of wool.
Woolly hat; can be worn in bed if it is really cold.

take three of everything to allow for washing; a pair of lightweight canvas shoes, to wear in the tent; cotton T-shirts, to wear on their own when it is hot, or wear two or three under a jumper if cold; socks, woolly ones for walking boots, lighter ones for other shoes; jeans or trousers, two pairs in wet or cold weather, but only one if it is hot; jumpers, two for cold weather, and one in hot weather as nights can still be cold; waterproof jacket, the type shown here packs into a pocket and dries easily.

T-shirts, three; very useful in any weather and easy to wash. Wear at night to save taking pyjamas.
Shorts.
Sandals; good for messing about.
Sun hat; important in hot sun.

Swimwear; take two costumes or pairs of trunks if you are likely to do a lot of swimming.
Canvas shoes; wear them when messing about around camp.

Sleeping equipment

To keep warm and sleep comfortably outdoors you need protective covering underneath as well as over you, because the ground is usually much colder at night.

The best way to keep warm is to use a sleeping bag. There are many different types, but the main things to consider when buying one are filling, quilting and fastenings.

Simple quilting

Wall quilting

Filling is down or man-made fibre. The second is usually cheaper and washable, but bulkier. The type of quilting affects the warmth. "Simple quilting" with stitching right through the walls of the bag is not as warm as "wall quilting," which gives an even filling throughout. Fastenings are zip or drawstring. Zips give a cold spot unless lined.

How to make a blanket bag

You may find a blanket bag useful when you first start to camp. Although it is rather bulky, it is cheaper than buying a sleeping bag. To make one, you need three blankets and three blanket pins.

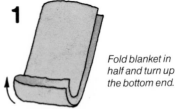

1

Fold blanket in half and turn up the bottom end.

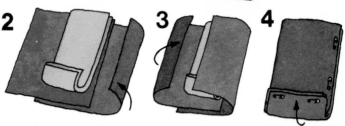

2

Fold bottom blanket over top blanket.

3

Fold middle blanket over both the others.

4

Fold up the bottom ends of the blankets and secure with blanket pins.

How to make a sleeping bag container

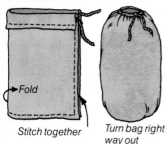

Fold

Stitch together

Turn bag right way out

If your sleeping bag is not sold with a container, you can either wrap it in a polythene bag or make a simple container as shown. Roll up your sleeping bag tightly and measure round it to find out how much material you need. Make sure you use waterproof material.

How to make a sheet lining bag

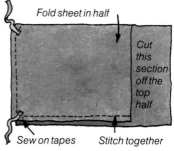

Fold sheet in half

Cut this section off the top half

Sew on tapes

Stitch together

A sheet liner will help to keep your sleeping bag clean inside. Make one from an old cotton sheet as shown. Sew tapes to the outside of the liner so that you can tie them with tapes in the bottom of your bag to stop the liner getting tangled round your feet.

Mattresses

A mattress makes sleeping on the ground more comfortable and is added protection against cold and damp.

Bubble

Foam

Bubble mattresses are made of a double sheet of plastic with rows of air bubbles in the middle. They are cheap and light to carry. Foam mattresses are also very light.

Inflatable mattresses need a lot of "puff" to blow them up unless you use a pump. They are heavier than bubble or foam and you need a repair kit in case of a puncture.

If you need a mattress but have not taken one with you, try stuffing newspaper, leaves or grass under the groundsheet. Be careful not to include sticks, which could tear the groundsheet.

Preparation and packing

Once you have practised living outdoors overnight, you will have a good idea of what you need for camping. What you actually take with you on a camping trip will depend on where you are going and the time of year. Make a checklist of things to take by thinking about the journey there, any special hobbies or activities you are likely to take part in, and any personal gear you will need.

Check your tent and all your other equipment to make sure it is in working order and nothing is lost. Finally, make sure your parents know exactly where you are going. Write your address down for them in case they want to contact you while you are away.

Travelling

Put things you need for the journey, such as map, compass, food and drink, at the top of your pack so you can find them easily.

Activities

Pack any gear you need for a special hobby such as fishing. Take a camera if you have one and don't forget your swimming things.

Labelling

Label everything you are taking with you so you know it is yours. Paint initials on mug and plates, and tie cotton round cutlery.

Personal gear

Don't forget personal gear: money, pen and notebook or diary, books, glasses, and any tablets or other special medicines you need.

When it is time to pack, collect everything together and lay it in piles on the floor. Cross things off your checklist as you do so. Make sure your sleeping bag and mattress are rolled up as tightly as possible, and all your clothes are rolled neatly.

There are no strict rules for packing but here are a few tips. If you go with a friend, share out equipment such as the tent and cooking utensils into two equal piles. Pack everything in polythene bags to keep it dry. Roll clothing or towels up tightly and put inside billy cans. Try to keep the stove and fuel separate from everything else so there is no danger of spoiling food or staining clothes.

MAKE SURE THAT OBJECTS DO NOT STICK INTO YOUR BACK

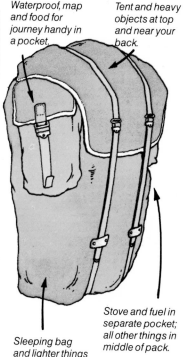

Waterproof, map and food for journey handy in a pocket.

Tent and heavy objects at top and near your back.

Stove and fuel in separate pocket; all other things in middle of pack.

Sleeping bag and lighter things at the bottom.

Rucksacks

There is a bewildering assortment of rucksacks. Which one you choose will depend on what you want to use it for and how much you want to spend. Most rucksacks are made of nylon or canvas. They have one or two main compartments, and various pockets on the outside. One compartment is generally thought to be more versatile and easier to pack.

Remember that you should always walk upright when you are loaded with a pack. Leaning forward will give you backache.

Shoulder straps

Many packs are made for use without a frame, and they have shoulder straps for carrying them by. They tend to be smaller than packs with frames.

Frames

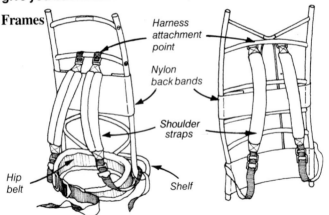

Harness attachment point

Nylon back bands

Shoulder straps

Hip belt

Shelf

Most larger packs are made so that they can be fixed onto frames of alloy tubing, which makes them easier to carry as the weight is better distributed. Frames have nylon back bands, and harnesses with wide padded shoulder straps. Some also have a hip belt, which may be padded. Some frames have a shelf at the bottom for carrying a sleeping mat or bag, or any other gear.

Buying a pack

Before you buy a pack, try it out with a load to see if it is comfortable. If you intend buying a pack with a frame, make sure nothing sticks into you or rubs against you. Remember that the larger the pack, the more you might be tempted to take with you. Check the points shown below to make sure that you are buying a reliable, well-made pack which will last.

1 Check the sac. Make sure all the seams are properly stitched and there is no sign of any frayed material. Check that all zips work.

2 Check that the frame is rigid. There should be no sharp edges and all the fixings should be secure.

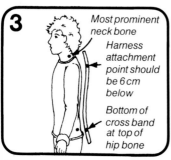

3
Most prominent neck bone

Harness attachment point should be 6 cm below

Bottom of cross band at top of hip bone

Check that the frame is the right size. If it is too long, it will rub against you and make you sore; if it is too short, it will put too much strain on your back as none of the weight will be carried on your hips. A good idea if you are still growing is to buy an adjustable frame.

TIP

Kitbag strapped to frame with belts

To save money, you can start with a pack that has a carrying harness, and buy a frame for it later on. Or you can start by buying a frame only, and making or buying something like a navy surplus kitbag to strap on.

Sleeping outdoors

If you go camping in warm, dry weather you can really enjoy the freedom of living outdoors and sleep without a tent. But remember that you will need a groundsheet under you, or a waterproofed sleeping bag, so that you do not get soaked by dew.

Bivouac shelters

If you prefer to have some protection over you, try using a large waterproof sheet to make a bivouac shelter. A sheet of thick polythene will do. It should be about 3 metres by 2½ metres. Sew loops of tape onto the edges for pegging them to the ground.

Tents

Tents are essential for winter camping or if the weather is cold or wet. A tent provides privacy, shelter from bad weather or a hot sun, and protection from insects and inquisitive or hungry animals.

The simplest and cheapest tents are the ridge and the bell tents. They are both popular for standing and lightweight camps.

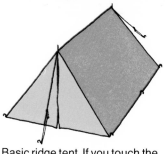

Basic ridge tent. If you touch the inside when it is raining it will leak, unless the material is coated.

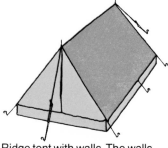

Ridge tent with walls. The walls give much more space around the edges of the tent.

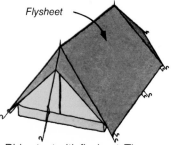

Flysheet

Ridge tent with flysheet. The flysheet helps to protect or insulate the tent from heat or cold, and stops rain leaking in.

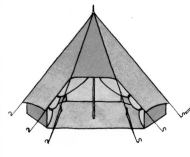

Bell tent with single pole. This is light to carry but the pole takes up some of the space inside.

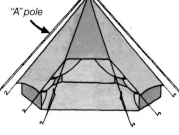

"A" pole

Bell tent with "A" pole. This has two poles on the outside instead of a single pole inside, so there is more space in the tent.

19

Choosing a tent

When choosing a tent you will have to think about the type you want, the materials it is made of, its size and weight, and whether any extras are included.

Study manufacturers' catalogues, then look around for any bargains in the shops: some tents are sold cheaply at the end of the season, or because they have been used as demonstration models.

The type of tent that you will probably find most useful is a ridge tent with a built-in groundsheet and a flysheet, like the one shown on this page. Do not make the mistake of getting a tent that is too heavy for you to carry. About 2.75 kilograms is a good weight for a two-person tent.

Fabric

Most tents are made of cotton or nylon. Cotton "breathes", so you do not get condensation inside the tent, but it is usually heavier and more expensive. It also stretches and shrinks with changes in the weather. Nylon tents are often cheaper, but nylon does not "breathe" as readily, so tents must have air vents.

Size

It is best to buy a two-person tent as you might want to share with a friend. Remember that your gear must fit inside the tent as well. A good size is 1.5 metres wide by two metres long and one metre high. You must be able to sit up and move around without touching the roof or walls.

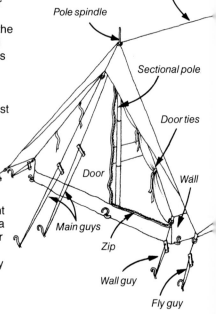

Ridge

Pole spindle

Sectional pole

Door ties

Door

Wall

Main guys

Zip

Wall guy

Fly guy

Colour

Tents are made in many different colours. Bright colours are easily seen from a distance and are often used in mountains, where mist and fog are a danger. In the country, green or brown tents may be preferred, to blend with the scenery. Remember that a light colour will be brighter inside.

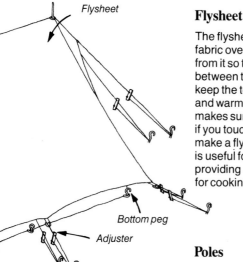

Flysheet

Bottom peg

Adjuster

Flysheet

The flysheet is an extra layer of fabric over the tent, held away from it so that there is a gap between the two layers. It helps to keep the tent cool in hot weather and warm in cold weather, and makes sure the tent does not leak if you touch it. You can also buy or make a flysheet extension, which is useful for storing equipment, providing a sheltered entrance, or for cooking in very bad weather.

Groundsheet

Groundsheets are made in a variety of waterproof materials. If the groundsheet is built-in, it should extend at least 10 centimetres up the tent walls.

Poles

Upright and ridge poles are usually made of wood, steel or metal alloy. Alloy is lightest and does not rust. Poles are in short sections which fit together; some pack inside one another to save space when carrying.

Setting up camp

When you arrive at your chosen camp site, you will have to decide exactly where to pitch your tent and which direction you want it to face.

Position your tent so that you have the most interesting view possible. If there is no obvious viewpoint, try pitching it so that you will be able to watch sunrise through the tent door. But be careful that the tent is not facing into strong wind, which could drive rain straight inside it.

If you are camping in summer, choose a place which catches the sun in the morning, but leaves the tent in the shade in the afternoon when you are likely to have had enough sun.

Once you have decided on the best position, go over the ground carefully. Remove any stones or twigs and stamp on any lumps.

If you do not bother to do this, you may regret it after a few nights of bad sleep, and you could even find holes in your groundsheet.

As soon as you have pitched the tent, fetch some drinking water. Set up and light your stove, and put some water on for a hot drink.

Unpack your sleeping bag and put it out to air. Put your spare shoes and the cooking utensils under the flysheet.

Set up a cooking area downwind from the tent and at least three metres away from it so there is no risk of fire. If you are using a stove,

choose or make a level place for it, so that pans do not slip off or fall over. Make sure it is sheltered from the wind.

Pitching a tent

Before you go camping, you should practise pitching your tent at home. Even if you are an experienced camper, you should practise if you have a new tent. A good idea is to put a sheet of polythene under the groundsheet. It protects the tent and keeps it clean.

The pictures on this page show how to pitch a ridge tent with two single poles and a built-in groundsheet. Those on the page opposite show how to pitch a ridge tent with two "A" poles and a separate groundsheet.

Pitching a ridge tent with built-in groundsheet

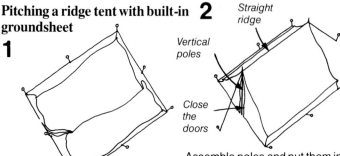

1

Peg base to ground, pegging out opposite corners first so that it is square and flat.

2

Straight ridge

Vertical poles

Close the doors

Assemble poles and put them in the spindle holes, rear one first. Lie them down and loosely peg out the main guys. Lift the poles upright and tighten the guys.

Wall guys should be about ⅔rds full length

3

Peg each corner wall guy in a straight line from the opposite pole and each middle guy from the centre of the ridge. Adjust guys so tent is taut and square.

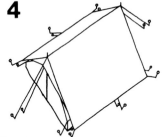

4

Place flysheet over tent, fitting holes over tent poles. Fix the main guys so the ridge is taut. Position pegs for side guys so flysheet is held away from tent.

Pitching a ridge tent with a separate groundsheet

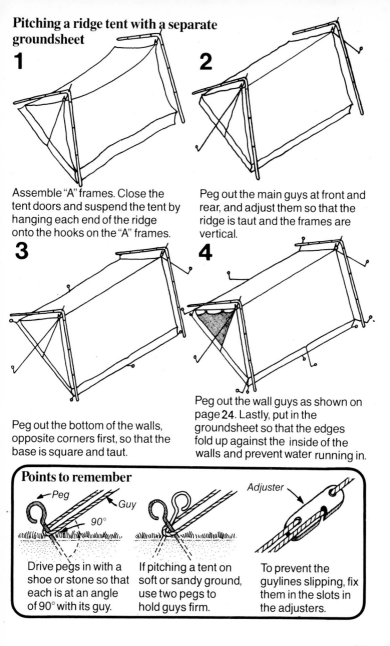

1

Assemble "A" frames. Close the tent doors and suspend the tent by hanging each end of the ridge onto the hooks on the "A" frames.

2

Peg out the main guys at front and rear, and adjust them so that the ridge is taut and the frames are vertical.

3

Peg out the bottom of the walls, opposite corners first, so that the base is square and taut.

4

Peg out the wall guys as shown on page 24. Lastly, put in the groundsheet so that the edges fold up against the inside of the walls and prevent water running in.

Points to remember

Peg — Guy — 90°

Drive pegs in with a shoe or stone so that each is at an angle of 90° with its guy.

If pitching a tent on soft or sandy ground, use two pegs to hold guys firm.

Adjuster

To prevent the guylines slipping, fix them in the slots in the adjusters.

Running a camp

Standing camps need some organization if they are to be enjoyed and the site left unscarred at the end of the camp. Apart from adequate supplies of food and water, you will have to think about washing your clothes and disposing of rubbish, and you will need to organize a toilet area. If you adopt a daily routine for basic essentials, they will take up very little time.

Prepare a menu before you go. If you plan ahead, you should only need to go shopping about every four days.

In fine weather, air the tent during the day by tying the doors back. Hang sleeping bags over the tent or a tree to air them too.

1 Rubbish

Keep rubbish in a polythene bag. Tie the bag to a tent guy or a tree near your cooking area so inquisitive animals can't get it.

Flatten empty cans by stamping on them so that they will take up less space in the rubbish bag.

If you have a fire you can burn most rubbish. Greasy water should be strained through bracken or grass, which can then be burnt.

BE ESPECIALLY CAREFUL WITH PLASTICS, ALUMINIUM FOIL AND GLASS, WHICH WON'T DECAY IF LEFT LYING AROUND. THEY ARE A DANGER TO ANIMALS, AND GLASS CAN START FIRES

How to make a toilet

To make a toilet you need to select a private place where you can dig a hole about half a metre deep. Pile the loose earth on one side and keep a trowel by it, so that each time the toilet is used some of the earth can be scattered back. Keep toilet paper in a polythene bag to keep it dry.

Washing clothes

Use separate bags for clean and dirty clothes. The dirty clothes bag can be kept under the flysheet. When you wash clothes, hang them out to dry on bushes or trees, or use string to make a washing line. If you use a double length of twisted string, you can tuck your washing into it and make do without pegs.

In general, wash clothes only when the weather is good, but if you are doing a lot of walking, wash your socks every day.

Washing

You may think that because you have the minimum of equipment and facilities at camp, it is a good opportunity to forget about such things as washing and bathing. Far from it! Since you will probably be involved in more strenuous activities than normal, washing is particularly important.

Do not waste drinking water by using it for washing, unless there is a plentiful supply. Take your washing gear to the nearest water source: a tap, river or lake, and wash there. It saves carrying water back to the tent. Do remember to use drinking water for cleaning your teeth.

Always wash your hands before handling food or preparing a meal, and after using the toilet.

Have a good all-over wash every three or four days and shampoo your hair at the same time. Make your own bath at camp if there is no lake or river nearby: dig a shallow hole and line it with a piece of polythene.

Put adhesive bandage over blisters after washing feet

Hardworking feet must be looked after carefully. Wash them thoroughly every day and dry well, especially between the toes. Use foot powder generously. Trim your toe nails regularly.

Flannel

Always rinse out your flannel after use, then put it out to dry on a bush, stone or stick. If it becomes smelly, you can boil it.

Soap

Keep soap dry in a container, otherwise you will end up with a slimy mess. If you put it down on the ground it will get covered with earth or grass.

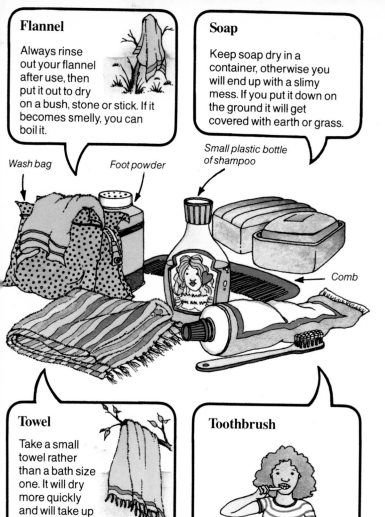

Wash bag

Foot powder

Small plastic bottle of shampoo

Comb

Towel

Take a small towel rather than a bath size one. It will dry more quickly and will take up less room in your pack.
Always hang it up to dry after use, but take it into the tent at night to prevent it getting damp with dew.

Toothbrush

If you forget to take your toothbrush or toothpaste with you, you can use your finger instead. Dip it in salt in place of toothpaste.

29

Cooking equipment

The equipment shown on this page is the minimum for two or three campers eating fresh cooked food. If you go lightweight camping, you will probably eat mostly dried, prepacked food and need less equipment.

Basic gear

Use a plate as a lid if you need one

Bottle opener on handle

Billy cans

You need two which fit or "nest" inside each other. They should be big enough to make a stew in and should be wide rather than deep.

Pan holder

Allows you to grip pans firmly without getting burnt. It can be carried inside billy cans.

Frying pan

Preferably non-stick with a folding handle, and the right size to fit on top of one of the billy cans so it can be used as a lid.

Wooden spatula

This will not scratch the frying pan. It can also be used for stirring and serving.

Can opener

A large one like this is best. It is easier to use and safer than the small ones, which leave ragged edges on tins.

Water bottle

Take a collapsible bottle big enough to hold $4\frac{1}{2}$ litres of water. The ones that have a flat base and can stand up are the easiest to fill.

Useful extras

Chopping board

A piece of plywood about 12 centimetres square is invaluable for cutting up vegetables.

Sharp knife

One about 15 centimetres long will make cutting bread and vegetables much easier.

Plastic strainer

Plastic is best because the flexible mesh makes it easier to pack. Use it for straining noodles, spaghetti, rice, tea and vegetables.

Plastic bowl with lid

Useful for mixing omelettes and pancake batter. Choose one that will fit inside your billy cans, and use it to keep food in while travelling.

Wire whisk

Saves time when making pancake batter and omelettes, and can be used to beat unwanted lumps out of things.

Personal gear

Label plates and cutlery

These are the things you will need for eating. Plastic is best as it does not chip or break.

Use plates to prepare food on as well as for eating, and use your mug for measuring.

Stoves

Cooking in the open air is fun, especially on a wood fire. But you may sometimes camp where there is no wood for fuel or where you are not allowed to light fires. Then you will need a stove to cook on.

There are many camping stoves to choose from. Different stoves use different kinds of fuel, so your choice will depend partly on the cost and availability of fuel. The type of camp will also help to decide which stove you should choose. Weight is most important for light-weight camping but the running cost could be a more important factor in standing camps.

Types of stove

The most popular types of stove use butane gas or paraffin, but there are also stoves that use petrol, methylated spirits or special tablets of solid fuel.

Solid fuel stoves are small and lightweight, but they do not give out as much heat as the others and are not very good for cooking. Their main purpose is for heating soup and hot drinks when you are out on day hikes.

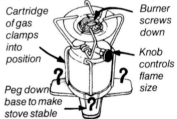

Cartridge of gas clamps into position

Burner screws down

Knob controls flame size

Peg down base to make stove stable

Gas cartridge stoves are good for lightweight camping as you do not need to carry a separate fuel container or funnel. The throw-away cartridge makes the stove easy to use but expensive.

Stove is ready for use on opening

Knob controls flame size

Large stable base

Grip handle for pans

Petrol stoves must be handled with care as the fuel can be dangerous. This stove is easy to use and folds away neatly, but petrol is an expensive fuel.

This **methylated spirit stove** is excellent for lightweight camping as it is a complete cooking set which packs into a small space and is light to carry.

How to use a paraffin pressure stove

Top ring

Burner

4. Prick **jet** to clean it, so that paraffin vapour can escape

1. Fill **tank** with fuel (not more than $\frac{3}{4}$ full)

2. Close **filler cap** tightly

3. Open **air valve**

5. Put priming fuel in **priming tray** and light it

6. Close **air valve** when fuel is almost burnt out

7. Give **pressure pump** one or two slow pumps: a small blue flame should appear on burner as paraffin vapour catches alight. Give a few harder pumps

Paraffin pressure stoves are the cheapest to run, but they need a second fuel, known as the primer, to start them working. The primer (methylated spirits or solid fuel) is used to quickly heat up the burner so that it is hot enough to vaporize the paraffin pumped up from the tank. The paraffin vapour burns and provides the heat for cooking.

If you pump too fast when you first light the stove, a sooty yellow flame will appear; liquid paraffin is being forced into the burner before it can vaporize. Turn off at once by opening the valve. Put more priming fuel in the tray and try again.

DO'S....		....& DON'TS
DO READ AND FOLLOW INSTRUCTIONS	DO KEEP FUEL AWAY FROM LIGHTED STOVE	DON'T COOK NEAR TENT. IT MIGHT CATCH FIRE
DO KEEP MATCHES IN A WATERPROOF TIN OR BOTTLE	DO CARRY FUEL IN A POLYTHENE BOTTLE. TAKE A FUNNEL	DON'T LEAVE EMPTY GAS CONTAINERS LYING AROUND, OR NEAR A FIRE – THEY MIGHT EXPLODE

33

Camp fires

REMEMBER! ALWAYS GET PERMISSION FROM LANDOWNER BEFORE MAKING A FIRE

DO'S....

DO POSITION DOWNWIND, 3 METRES FROM TENT

DO CLEAR ANYTHING THAT MIGHT CATCH FIRE

DO COLLECT ENOUGH WOOD BEFORE YOU START

DO KEEP WATER OR A STICK HANDY TO PUT OUT FIRE

DO MAKE SURE YOU PUT OUT FIRE AFTER USE

...& DON'TS

DON'T PUT UPWIND FROM TENT, OR IN A WINDY PLACE

DON'T POSITION UNDER BUSHES OR TREES—THEY MAY CATCH FIRE

DON'T POSITION ON LEAF MOULD OR THICK PINE NEEDLES

DON'T EVER LEAVE A FIRE UNATTENDED

Preparing the ground

1 On grass

Cut out turf. Try to keep each piece whole by rolling it back.

2

Store turf flat. Put it upside down in a cool damp place.

3

Line edges of hole with logs or stones to protect grass.

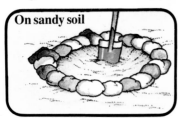

On sandy soil

Dig a shallow pit and surround it with stones. Do not use flint or river stones, they can explode.

On wet ground

Make a bed of stones, sand or green sticks, which don't burn readily, to build your fire on.

Search trees and bushes for dead twigs and branches, which are leafless and break off easily. This wood is dry and burns well. Dead wood from the ground is often too damp to burn.

If the sticks you collect are too long for use, break them up as shown. Nick each stick on opposite sides with a penknife, and then snap it sharply over a log or rock at the nicked point, using your foot.

Laying a fire

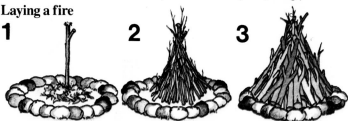

1 **2** **3**

Start by pushing a forked stick into the ground in the centre of your fireplace. Add dry grass, lightly crumpled paper or a strip of birch bark around it and then build up a tent of dry twigs, gradually increasing their size.

If you have a very big log, build a fire around the middle of it and push the ends in as it burns. You can also do this with two logs, one leant over the other.

TIP

If you do not have paper, bark or dry grass for a fire, cut shavings on a dry stick. Use this as your central fire stick, building a tent of twigs around it.

Supporting your cooking pan

A well-built fire is one in which the outside wood keeps falling into the burning centre. The fire is continually being refuelled, and any wood that is slightly damp will dry out first on the outside.

Fires built for cooking do not need to be big. Large fires waste fuel and are more difficult to put out when you have finished using them. The pictures below show several ways to cook over a fire.

Use two large logs or stones and rest two metal bars or green sticks across them to support your pan. Place a piece of metal mesh over the logs for barbecuing.

Dig a pit for a trench fire and rest your billy on the edges. The pit should slope down to a depth of about 20 centimetres at one end, for the fire. Lay the fuel lengthwise.

Hang a billy over the fire on a notched stick, supported by a crossbar and forked sticks placed either side of the fire, as shown.

Build a fire around two flat stones on which you can then rest your billy.

Hang a billy from a stick held in place by stones as shown.

Or raise the stick over the fire by using two other forked sticks.

Food and storage

Eat on day of purchase

Fresh meat and fish should always be cooked and eaten on the day they are bought. If you buy frozen food you will need to eat it the same day.

Eat within a few days

Bacon and other meat containing preservatives can be kept a bit longer. Eggs and cheese, and fresh fruit and vegetables will also keep for several days.

Keep as long as you like

Many foods can be kept almost indefinitely. Take the following with you: flour, sugar, breakfast cereal, tea, coffee, squash, herbs, salt and pepper, and cooking oil. Also take with you as much of the following as you have room for: canned meat and fish; dried foods such as rice, pasta, lentils, fruit and nuts, and milk powder; packet sauce mixes and soup, and freeze-dried vegetables.

Storing food

Stones

Billy can

FOOD

Try these ideas to keep food fresh, and safe from insects and animals. Keep fruit and vegetables in a string bag hung from a tree. Dig a hole in the ground for food such as cheese and sausages; cover it with greenery, and leave a sign so no-one steps in it. Stand milk in water with a damp cloth over. If there is a stream near, put food in a plastic bag tied to the bank.

Cooking on a stove

TIPS

1 Wind wastes a lot of heat. Make a shield of sticks or stones to protect your stove, or use a bag stretched over two sticks in the ground. See also page 55.

2 Before you start cooking, plan the best order of preparation for a meal. Remember that you only have one stove, two billies, and a frying pan.

3 Meat and vegetables cook more quickly if cut up small. Cook all the vegetables for a meal together in one billy.

Cover billy with a cloth

4 Begin by half-cooking vegetables, pasta or rice. Keep them warm and they will be ready by the time the sauce or meat is cooked.

Rice and vegetable salad

5 Cook extra helpings of vegetables, noodles or rice. Eat them the next day with a sauce, as a salad, or fried.

6 Whenever the stove is alight but not being used to cook, such as between two courses of a meal, use it to boil water for washing up or a hot drink afterwards.

Sterilizing water

If you can't get tap water, you must sterilize water before using it for cooking or drinking. Filter it through cloth or two layers of nylon stocking until clear, then boil it or use purifying tablets. If using tablets, you need to add special tablets afterwards to improve the taste.

A filling meal for two people

This page shows how to plan and cook a filling meal for two people. The menu is: soup, noodles with tomato sauce, and pancakes. You will need:

For the soup: a half litre packet of soup.

For the main course: 200 grams of pasta; a small tin of tomato puree; an onion; a mug of milk (can be made from milk powder); 3 tablespoons of oil or butter; pinch of salt and pepper.

For the pancakes: an egg; 3 tablespoons of flour; a mug of milk; small amount of margarine; pinch of salt; jam, or lemon and sugar to put on cooked pancakes.

Light stove. Put on large billy full of water. Cover.

Mix flour, egg and salt. Add milk slowly. Beat to smooth batter.

Use some of the hot water to make soup in second billy.

While soup is cooking, chop up onion. Open tin of tomato puree.

Drink soup. Boil water left in first billy. Add pasta and salt.

Take half-cooked pasta off stove. Fry onion in oil in soup billy.

Add milk, tomato puree, salt and pepper. Stir until sauce is hot.

Test pasta by cutting. If hard inside, cook a little longer.

Drain pasta. Serve with sauce and eat.

Heat a teaspoon of margarine in frying pan. Pour in ½ cup of batter.

Cook for about a minute. Turn over when underside is golden.

When cooked on both sides, eat with lemon juice and sugar, or jam.

Camp fire cooking

Food cooked over a camp fire has a delicious flavour. You must let the fire burn down to red coals before you start cooking; flames only burn and blacken food. If you are going to use a fire for grilling, you will need green sticks for cooking utensils. Food can also be cooked in the ashes. It is usually best wrapped in aluminium foil to keep in the flavour and juices.

Cooking on sticks

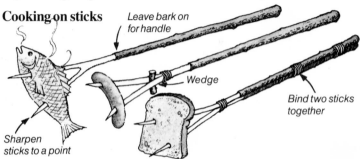

Leave bark on for handle

Wedge

Bind two sticks together

Sharpen sticks to a point

Cook fish, sausages and toast on sticks of green wood with the bark stripped off. Use forked sticks so the food does not drop off into the fire. If you can't find a forked stick, make one by splitting a large stick for part of its length and wedging it open with a piece of wood. Or bind two sticks together at one end.

Kebab

Dough twist

Marshmallow

Tongs

Marshmallows, kebabs and twists can be cooked on straight sticks. Make twists by adding water to a mug of flour to make a stiff dough. Toast on a stick. Fill with jam to eat.

Tongs are useful for picking up stray embers and any food that falls off sticks while cooking. Make them from green wood, by lashing together forked and curved sticks.

Cooking in foil in the ashes

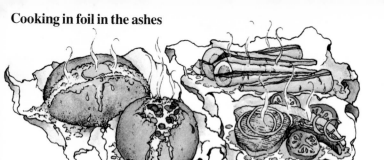

Potatoes Scrub, wrap in foil and bury in hot ashes for half an hour to an hour, depending on size. Eat with butter or cheese.

Apples Cut out core and fill the centre with currants and sugar. Wrap in foil and bury in ashes for 25-45 minutes.

Parsnips Peel or scrub, and cut into "sticks". Wrap up in foil, dotting with butter as you do so, and cook in ashes for 30-40 minutes.

Chops and **steaks** Wrap in foil with tomato and mushrooms and a pinch of salt, and bury in ashes for 30 minutes.

More methods

Heat a flat stone in the fire until it is nearly red hot. Dust any ash off it, brush with oil and use to cook meat and fish on.

Make a barbecue by supporting a piece of metal mesh on logs over hot coals. Brush the mesh with oil before you put food on it.

To cook an egg, prick a hole in one end and stand in hot ashes for ten minutes. Or, cut the top off an orange, scoop out the flesh and cook egg in "shell".

Cook a stew overnight in a billy stood in hot ashes. Make sure you cover the billy with a lid or plate and bank the ashes up round it almost to the top. Boil up the next day before eating.

Clearing up after a meal

After eating, close all food containers and put them back in their place so you will know where to find them again. Dispose of rubbish, as shown on page 26, so it does not attract insects or become a danger to animals. Collect dirty dishes together and have plenty of hot water ready for washing them.

Wipe your plate with bread when you finish a meal. It will fill you up if you are still hungry, and make washing up easier.

Dishes become more difficult to clean if they are left standing, so wash up straight away. Use the largest billy to wash up in.

Brush

Washing up liquid in plastic bottle

Dishcloth

Pan scourer   Washing soda crystals

You will need the items shown above for washing up, but don't use the scourer on non-stick pans. You may find washing soda crystals more convenient to use than liquid, as a small quantity can be kept in a plastic bag and you only need one spoonful at a time.

Dry everything with a tea towel. Start with the plates so that other things can be stacked on top as shown here.

When you finish, hang tea towels out to dry. Put things away so that they are always in the same place and can be found again.

How to put out a fire

If you cook on a fire, use dirty washing up water to put it out. Sprinkle water over fire with your fingers.

Then use a green stick to spread out the smouldering embers a little, so they will cool off more quickly.

Sprinkle more water onto the remains of the fire. Do not leave it until you are quite sure it is out.

Things to make

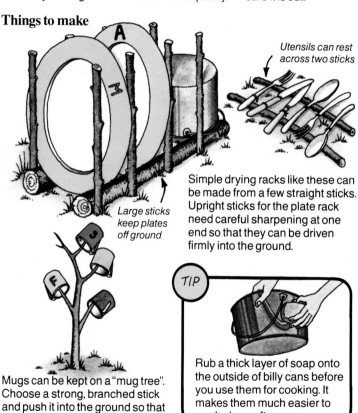

Utensils can rest across two sticks

Large sticks keep plates off ground

Simple drying racks like these can be made from a few straight sticks. Upright sticks for the plate rack need careful sharpening at one end so that they can be driven firmly into the ground.

Mugs can be kept on a "mug tree". Choose a strong, branched stick and push it into the ground so that it stands firmly upright.

TIP

Rub a thick layer of soap onto the outside of billy cans before you use them for cooking. It makes them much easier to wash clean after use.

43

Things to do

July 12th
sunny and quite warm.
Cornflakes, sausages + bacon
for breakfast

Did some tracking
in the woods.
Found a Pheasant's
feather, part of
the shell of a
thrush's egg,
and saw
these
footprints

Squirrel
footprints

Bread, cheese, salad + fruit for
lunch.
Played football in a field
nearby, and found this
butterfly wing

Red Admiral
Butterfly
wing

Went into Bray village - lovely
old houses
and shops.
(this is part
of a postcard)

Risotto for
supper. Played
cards.

Whenever you go camping, it is interesting and useful to keep a diary. You will have hours of fun looking back over it long after the camp has ended. A hard-backed notebook is best. Get into the habit of writing in it every evening, and make sketches too. Note down the weather, the food you have eaten, where you went and the route you followed, and what you saw. Anything new you found out or want to find out more about should also be included.

In bad weather

Take with you some playing cards, a pocket chess or draughts set, dice, books, and a selection of pencils, colouring pens and paper.

Use the time to clean and repair clothes and equipment. Then try inventing and making new gadgets which might be useful at camp.

During the day

Get up early to watch the sun rise. Animals are more likely to be seen earlier too, especially near water where they go to drink.

Look for animal tracks, and signs such as burrows, droppings, hair or feathers. Collect seashells or leaves, but do not pick flowers.

If you get tired of games such as football, try competitions such as seeing who can skim a small stone furthest across the sea or a lake.

Try tracking: one person sets off 20 minutes before the others and leaves a trail for them to follow. Use signs such as those above.

At night

Go for a night walk. Keep quiet so that you will hear any noises made by animals that are active at night. Try spotting stars.

WARNING! USE A TORCH IN THE TENT, NOT A CANDLE, THE TENT MIGHT CATCH FIRE

Sit round a camp fire and sing, tell stories or play charades. Discuss and plan what to do and where to go the next day.

Striking camp

When it is time to go home or move onto another site, you will have to dismantle your camp, pack, and clear up the site. This is known as "striking camp". It is best to follow the routine shown here, packing first and taking down the tent last. This way you will still keep fairly dry if it rains while you are striking camp.

After your last meal, wash up and prepare food and drink for the journey. If you used a stove, leave it to cool, then empty and clean it.

Collect all your things together outside the tent, or inside if it is wet. Check them against your list to see that you have everything.

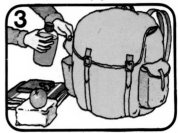

Pack everything. Put tickets, food, drink, money, maps, jacket and anything else you may need on the journey at the top or in pockets.

When you have packed everything except the tent, clear up the site. Pick up any remaining rubbish and burn it or put it in the farmer's dustbin. If you can't do either of these, bury it or take it home. Fill in any holes you made for a fireplace or toilet. If turf was removed, replace it, stamp it down and water thoroughly.

5

Sweep out the tent. Take it down by reversing the order of the stages you followed for pitching it.

6

Make sure you pull up all the pegs. In hard ground, you may need to use a piece of string as shown, or a peg puller (see page 53).

7

Fold up guy ropes carefully and tie each one in a large knot so that they do not get tangled.

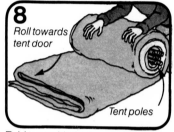

8

Roll towards tent door

Tent poles

Fold tent with the groundsheet outside and wipe over. Fold up the flysheet and lay on top. Dismantle poles and roll tent up round them, rolling towards the tent entrance so that no air is trapped inside.

9

Always leave a site exactly as you found it. Take a last look round to make sure nothing is left behind; you will be surprised at how often you discover an odd piece of washing.

Arriving home

As soon as possible after arriving home, check over all your equipment and clothing. When you unpack, put things you have not used in a separate pile and see if there is anything you need not take next time. When you have done this, make a new check-list of equipment. Include on it anything you needed but did not take.

Wash or air your sleeping bag and then store it lightly folded. Make sure all your clothes are washed, and your sleeping bag liner if you used one.

Clean your shoes or walking boots. Brush or scrape dirt off them, then treat with boot oil or wax, rubbing it in with an old cloth.

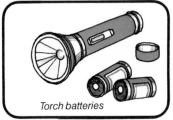

Torch batteries

If you do not use your torch at home, take the batteries out before putting it away so that they do not rot it.

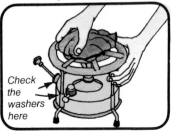

Check the washers here

If you used a stove, make sure no fuel is left in it, then clean and polish it. Look for signs of wear and replace parts such as washers if necessary.

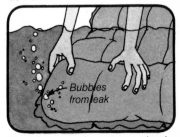

Bubbles from leak

If you have an air mattress, check that it has not sprung a leak by dipping it, a bit at a time, in a bath or basin of water. Look for bubbles which show where there is a hole.

Air your tent to make sure it is dry. Wipe pole joints with an oily cloth and clean pegs, straightening any that are bent. Check your tent and rucksack for signs of wear.

When you have finished cleaning and repairing your equipment, put it all together in a box and store in a dry place. You can then find it easily when you want it again.

Repairs

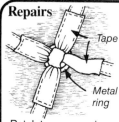

Tape

Metal ring

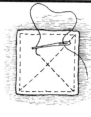

"D" ring

Patch tears round the spindle holes by pushing lengths of tape through the metal ring and stitching both sides.

Mend a tear in the tent wall with a square of fabric, larger than the tear. Turn the edges under and sew on.

If a guy is torn off, patch the tear, then sew a tape round with a metal "D" ring on it, to which the guy can be attached.

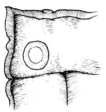

A hole in the groundsheet can be patched underneath with adhesive carpet tape, or by using a bicycle puncture kit.

A bicycle puncture kit is also useful for repairing a hole in your air mattress.

If you use the tent a lot, you should treat it every year with waterproofing agent, which you can buy in a spray can.

49

Weather

The site you choose for pitching your tent, the food you eat and the way you store it, the clothes you wear and your daily camp routine all depend on the weather. These pages show some tips and points to remember for camping in different kinds of weather.

Hot weather

If it is very hot you could sleep in the open instead of in your tent. You might find it more comfortable in a hammock.

Pitch your tent in shade, if possible in a position where it will catch any breeze. Keep tent doors and any air vents open.

Hot weather is much more tiring. If it is very hot, take salt tablets with you. Remember to take calamine lotion too, in case of sunburn.

Keeping food fresh is much more difficult in hot weather. If there is a stream near the camp, you can use it as a larder (see page 37).

Wet weather

Tents without flysheets are likely to leak if touched inside. You can stop leaks by dripping candle wax onto the leak on the outside.

Pitch your tent on the highest ground available so that water will drain away from your site and not towards it.

Wear sandals and shorts rather than shoes, socks and trousers. You will be more comfortable if you get soaked.

Always pack all your equipment in plastic bags so that, even if the tent leaks, your things will not get wet.

If the groundsheet is not built-in, it is a good idea to fold it back from the door so it does not get wet and muddy.

If it rains so much that water starts to run under the tent, dig a small trench around it on three sides to drain the water away. Make sure you fill the trench in before leaving the site.

Cold weather

Pitch your tent on a site sheltered from the wind. Keep the doors and air vents closed.

In extremely cold weather, a sleeping bag liner can be filled with dry leaves or hay and used as a mattress or a cover. The ground gets much colder at night, so you need plenty of protection under as well as over you.

Keep warm at night by wearing more clothes. Socks, underwear, a pullover and even a woolly hat will keep you warm in bed.

Build a reflector fire

If it is very cold, open the tent doors and build a reflector fire about a metre in front of the tent. This kind of fire is built with a barrier behind it so that heat is reflected in one direction, in this case, towards the tent. The barrier is usually a small wall of logs, but almost any large flat object will do. See page 36 for how to make a fire safely.

Extra tips

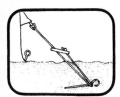

If you are pitching your tent on sandy soil, bury the tent pegs in the soil, so they are anchored as firmly as possible.

Tent pegs are quite easy to make. Find a forked stick and shave one end off to a point so it can be driven into the ground.

Boots are best kept outside the tent to air them. Put them upside down on sticks like this, so air can circulate all round.

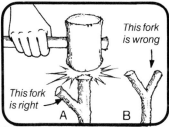

When you use a forked stick to make a camp gadget, choose one like A, which can be driven into the ground easily. Fork B will be no use, it will probably split.

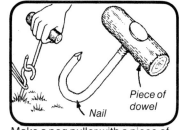

Make a peg puller with a piece of wood, dowel is ideal, and a long nail. Drill a hole in the wood, then push the nail through and bend it with a pair of pliers.

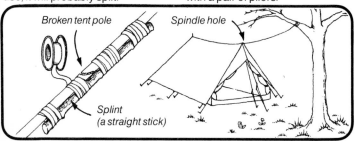

If a tent pole breaks, bind it firmly to a splint with string or tape from a first aid kit. Or use string to hang the tent from a tree: thread one end of the string down through the spindle hole and tie it round a small object such as a peg. Tie the other end up to the tree.

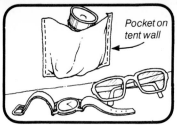

A pocket sewn on to the tent wall is useful for keeping a pair of glasses, a watch, or a torch handy. It should be made of a similar fabric to the tent.

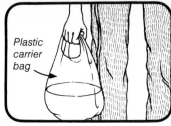

Use a large plastic carrier bag as an extra water carrier. Check the bag over first to make sure it is not the type with holes in. Never fill it more than half full.

If you are caught in the rain without a waterproof jacket, you can use a large polythene bag. Cut a narrow hole along the bottom edge of the bag near one end, and wear this end over your head.

Take an old pillow case with you to make a pillow. You can stuff it with spare clothing, such as jumpers and T-shirts, or anything else you can find like leaves, grass or straw.

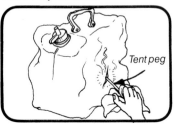

You can seal a hole in a polythene container such as a water carrier by using a tent peg. Heat the peg until it is hot enough to melt the polythene, then smear it across the hole. Hold the hot peg with a cloth.

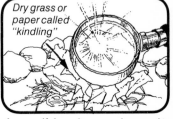

A magnifying glass can be used to light a camp fire on a clear sunny day if you run out of matches. Hold it at an angle so that it catches the sun's rays and directs them onto kindling in a fireplace.

An extra cooking pot can be made from a large can. Punch two holes just below the rim and thread wire through for a handle.

If you collect wood for a fire, stack it under a bush or up against a tree. If it rains, the wood will stay dry.

Make a wind shield for cooking from four bicycle spokes or pieces of garden cane, and a strip of fabric about a metre long. See also page 38.

Emergency kit

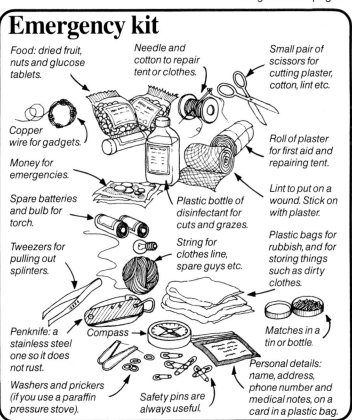

Food: dried fruit, nuts and glucose tablets.

Needle and cotton to repair tent or clothes.

Small pair of scissors for cutting plaster, cotton, lint etc.

Copper wire for gadgets.

Money for emergencies.

Roll of plaster for first aid and repairing tent.

Spare batteries and bulb for torch.

Plastic bottle of disinfectant for cuts and grazes.

Lint to put on a wound. Stick on with plaster.

Tweezers for pulling out splinters.

String for clothes line, spare guys etc.

Plastic bags for rubbish, and for storing things such as dirty clothes.

Penknife: a stainless steel one so it does not rust.

Compass

Matches in a tin or bottle.

Washers and prickers (if you use a paraffin pressure stove).

Safety pins are always useful.

Personal details: name, address, phone number and medical notes, on a card in a plastic bag.

Recipes

tbsp = tablespoon   tsp = teaspoon

Plan your menu so that you have a good breakfast and evening meal. Sandwiches or salad will do midday. Try the following ideas:
Breakfast. Cereal or muesli; scrambled, boiled or fried egg with fried bacon and tomato; fried or eggy bread; kipper; sausages.

Midday. Salad; sandwiches with cheese, sausage, paté, hard-boiled egg, jam, cold meat, sardines, or tuna; crisps; dried fruit and nuts.
Evening meal. Soup; curry and rice; omelette; stew with dumplings; risotto; kebabs; pasta with sauce; rice salad; beefburgers; fruit or jelly.

Muesli (for one person)

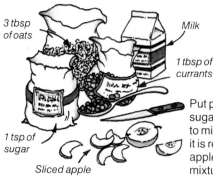

3 tbsp of oats

Milk

1 tbsp of currants

1 tsp of sugar

Sliced apple

Put porridge oats, currants and sugar in a mug or bowl. Stir round to mix up, then add some milk and it is ready to eat. Try adding sliced apple and nuts to the muesli mixture as well.

Eggy bread (for two)

1 tbsp of cooking oil

1 tbsp of milk

4 slices of bread

Pinch of salt and pepper

3 eggs

Mix eggs, milk, salt and pepper together in a billy. Put the bread in this mixture and leave it to soak for a few minutes. Heat the cooking oil in the frying pan and fry each slice of bread on both sides until it is golden brown.

Omelette (for two)

1 tbsp of oil

3 tbsp milk

4 eggs

Salt and pepper

Omelette fillings

Mix eggs, milk, salt and pepper in a mug with a fork. Heat the oil in the frying pan, pour in half the mixture and cook until set. Fold in half to serve. Try filling the omelette with ham, cheese, mushrooms or any other cooked vegetables.

Beefburgers (for two)

Pinch of salt and pepper

250 grams of minced beef

Medium onion

One egg

One slice of bread

Beat the egg in a bowl and add the slice of bread to soak it up. Chop the onion finely, then mix it thoroughly with the minced beef, salt and pepper, and egg-soaked bread. Divide mixture in two, roll into balls and flatten. Fry burgers for about ten minutes each side.

Macaroni cheese (for two)

Large mugful of macaroni

Packet of cheese sauce mix

2 tomatoes, sliced

Grated cheese

Cook the macaroni in boiling salted water for ten minutes, until it is soft. Make up the cheese sauce, following the instructions on the packet. Drain the macaroni and mix it into the sauce. Top with tomato and cheese to serve.

Rice salad (for two)

Mug of rice

4 tbsp of oil

1 tbsp of currants

Pinch of salt and pepper

Juice of a lemon

Small onion

Chopped vegetables

Handful of peanuts

Cook rice in a large billy of boiling salted water for about fifteen minutes, until just soft. Drain and leave to go cold. Chop up or grate small quantities of any vegetables available and add to cold rice. Mix together the oil, lemon juice, salt and pepper in a mug. Pour over the salad and mix carefully with a spoon handle to keep the ingredients whole.

Potato curry (for two)

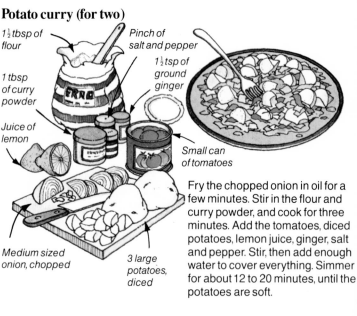

$1\frac{1}{2}$ tbsp of flour

Pinch of salt and pepper

$1\frac{1}{2}$ tsp of ground ginger

1 tbsp of curry powder

Juice of lemon

Small can of tomatoes

Medium sized onion, chopped

3 large potatoes, diced

Fry the chopped onion in oil for a few minutes. Stir in the flour and curry powder, and cook for three minutes. Add the tomatoes, diced potatoes, lemon juice, ginger, salt and pepper. Stir, then add enough water to cover everything. Simmer for about 12 to 20 minutes, until the potatoes are soft.

Instant stew (for two)

Can of meat

Packet of dried vegetables (or left-overs)

Large packet of vegetable soup

Dumplings

3 tbsp of flour

Large potato (200 grams) peeled and cut up

Pinch of salt

Make up the vegetable soup, following the instructions on the packet. Add the canned meat and the vegetables, and cook together. To make the dumplings, first boil the potatoes until soft, then mash them. Mix together with the flour and salt until you get a thick paste. Roll into small balls, dip in flour and drop into boiling stew. Cook for about ten minutes.

Risotto (for two)

½ mug of rice

Mug of water

1 tbsp of oil

½ packet of soup

1 tbsp of butter

100 grams of mushrooms, sliced

2 tomatoes, sliced (or small can)

Medium onion

Heat oil and butter together in the frying pan and fry rice until golden brown. Add chopped onion and fry for a few minutes. Then add mushrooms and tomatoes. Mix the packet soup with cold water and add to the rice and vegetables. Cook, stirring gently, until the rice has absorbed all the liquid.

Knots

There are a great variety of knots, designed for all sorts of different purposes. These pages show only a few of the many you will come across.

All of them are knots which might be useful when you are camping, either for mending things or for making camp gadgets.

Clove hitch

This is a good knot for tying something to a post or pole.

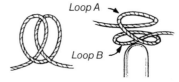

Loop A

Loop B

Make two loops like this.

Place loop A over loop B.

Slip the loops over the post.

Pull both ends of rope tightly.

Heaving line bend

Use this knot for tying together two ropes of different thickness.

Sling

This is the best way to carry a can or bucket without a handle.

Place the can on the string.

Tie the ends of the string over each other on top.

Pull tie apart and slip over edges of can.

Tighten string round can and tie ends for handle.

Whipping

This is used for binding things together firmly and neatly. You might use it on a loose knife handle.

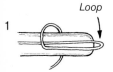

1

Loop

Place cord round object, making a long loop as shown above.

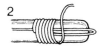

2

Bind cord neatly round and round, working from left to right.

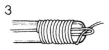

3

When you have finished, put the end of the cord through the loop.

4

B

Pull on the end of the cord labelled B.

5

This pulls the other end under the binding.

6

Cut off the remaining ends of the cord.

How to make a rope ladder

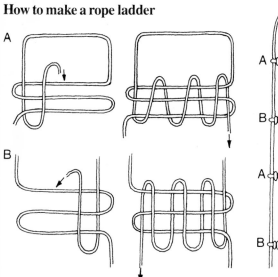

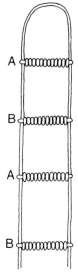

Book list

Better Camping. Alan Ryalls & Roger Marchant (Kaye & Ward). A good book for beginners, illustrated with lots of clear black and white photographs, and including sections on cycle and canoe camping.

Camping for Young People. Anthony Greenbank (Piccolo). A good inexpensive paperback, easy to follow, with tables and line drawings.

The Spur Book of Camping. Terry Brown & Rob Hunter (Spur). A useful book for beginners of any age, illustrated with line drawings. Many useful booklets on camping and other outdoor activities are published by The Scout Association, including: *Enjoy Camping.* Doug Mountford. *The Scout Standard* and *The Advanced Scout Standard.* Steve Scholes.

Useful addresses

The Camping Club of Great Britain and Ireland, 11 Grosvenor Place, London SW1. The club has a Camping Club Youth section for young people between the ages of 12 and 17. All members of this section are given a useful booklet on joining called *Fundamentals of Good Camping.* This has small sections on map reading and first aid, as well as lots of notes on camp equipment and behaviour. Members are taught camping skills by voluntary youth leaders and can then take a test to show that they can camp efficiently and safely on their own. A programme of youth activities is organized by the club throughout the year, and activities take place every weekend in summer.

Youth Hostels Association, Trevelyan House, St Stephen's Hill, St Alban's, Hertfordshire. YHA shops sell equipment and clothing for all kinds of outdoor activities including camping, and can advise on the right gear for your needs.

The Girl Guides Association, 17-19 Buckingham Palace Road, London SW1.

The Scout Association, Baden-Powell House, Queen's Gate, London SW7. Camping equipment can be bought at Scout Shops and a few shops hire out tents.

To find out about branches of these organizations in your area, or for any other information about camping and camping books, ask at your local library.

Index